BEAUTIFUL
ATHLETE

Love-Always,
Grandpa and
Wa-Wa   "2013"

SPORTS
GIRL

MAGGIE'

COMPETITIVE
VOLLEYBALL
FOR GIRLS

CLAUDIA B. MANLEY

the rosen publishing group's
**rosen
central**

Published in 2001 by The Rosen Publishing Group, Inc.
29 East 21st Street, New York, NY 10010

Library of Congress Cataloging-in-Publication Data

Manley, Claudia B.
Competitive volleyball for girls / by Claudia B. Manley. — 1st ed.
p. cm. — (Sportsgirl)
Includes bibliographical references (p.) and index.
ISBN 0-8239-3404-7 (lib. bdg.)
1. Volleyball for girls. 2. Volleyball for women. I. Title. II. Series.
GV1015.4.W66 M36 2001
796.325'082—dc21

00-012210

Manufactured in the United States of America

Contents

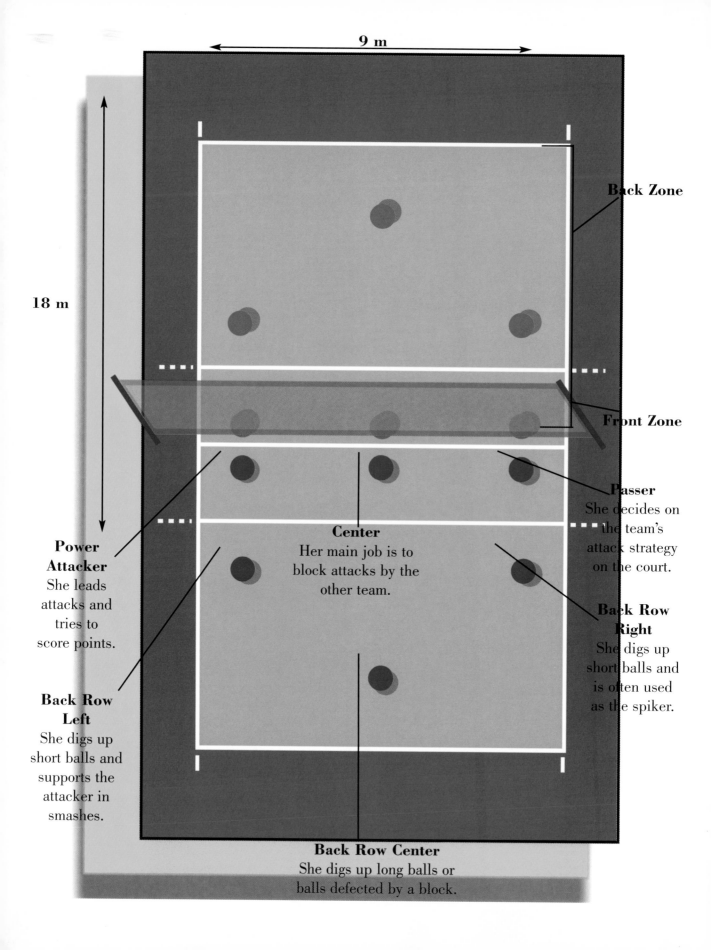

9 m

18 m

Back Zone

Front Zone

Passer
She decides on
the team's
attack strategy
on the court.

**Power
Attacker**
She leads
attacks and
tries to
score points.

Center
Her main job is to
block attacks by the
other team.

**Back Row
Right**
She digs up
short balls and
is often used
as the spiker.

**Back Row
Left**
She digs up
short balls and
supports the
attacker in
smashes.

Back Row Center
She digs up long balls or
balls defected by a block.

Introduction

"No person in the United States shall, on the basis of sex, be excluded from participation in, be denied the benefits of, or be subjected to discrimination under any education program or activity receiving Federal financial assistance . . ."

The above is from Title IX, which is part of the Education Amendments that Congress passed in 1972. It deals specifically with discrimination against girls and women in federally funded educational institutions. When it was first passed, it attracted little controversy. Guidelines on how to enforce it weren't even issued until 1974, and even then little was done to carry out these orders. Though it did make some headway in helping girls receive more opportunities in sports, a Supreme Court ruling in 1984 effectively took the wind out of Title IX's sails. In the ruling *Grove City v. Bell*, the court said that schools didn't have to follow Title IX guidelines in programs that didn't receive federal funding directly.

This included athletics. That is, if a school did not directly receive funding for athletics, the institution did not have to abide by Title IX in its athletic programs.

Many people were outraged. They disagreed with the Supreme Court decision. Finally, in 1988, Congress passed the Civil Rights Restoration Act, over the veto of then-president Ronald Reagan. This overturned the *Grove City* ruling and stated that sex discrimination was against the law throughout any educational institution if it received any federal funding. This meant that even if a school's sports program didn't receive federal funds, but other programs in the school did, the sports program still had to follow Title IX.

In practical terms, Title IX means that educational institutions must provide as much funding and resources for female athletes as they do for male athletes. It doesn't mean that if a university has a boy's football team, they have to have one for girls, too. It does mean, however, that the amount of money spent on boys' athletics has to be proportionally the same as that spent on girls' athletics.

Women and girls have since benefited greatly from Title IX. Many women Olympians and professional athletes credit the passage and enforcement of Title IX for their success in athletics. This should not be surprising, considering that the percentage of girls participating in high school sports rose from 36 percent before Title IX and to above 50 percent since.

Title IX had a tremendous impact on the sport of women's volleyball. The resources provided for women's volleyball after the passage of Title IX enabled the sport to grow in popularity. It also helped many high school players afford a college or university education by making many more athletic scholarships available to women. Support for volleyball has given girls of all ages opportunities to get into the game and has made volleyball the third most popular sport for high school girls.

1 An Introduction to Volleyball

Volleyball was invented in 1895 in Holyoke, Massachusetts. An instructor at a YMCA, William G. Morgan, wanted a game that combined elements of basketball, tennis, baseball, and handball. The sport was originally called mintonette, but the action of volleying the ball back and forth over the net gave it its current name, volleyball.

Since then the popularity of the sport has continued to rise. Indoor volleyball made its debut at the 1964 Olympics in Tokyo, and beach volleyball was recently made a medal sport at the 1996 Olympics in Atlanta. In recent years, it has ranked third among the most popular sports for girls in junior and senior high school. More than 24 million Americans—men, women, and children—play volleyball in the United States today.

The women's game has come a long way since 1895, as well. In 1933, the

Beach volleyball made its Olympic debut at the 1996 games in Atlanta, Georgia.

earliest reference for teaching the game to women, *Volleyball for Women* by Katherine M. Montgomery, was published. In 1952, the first Women's World Championships were held in Moscow, and with the inclusion of volleyball in the 1964 Olympics, it was clear that women's volleyball was here to stay.

The 1970s was a productive decade for women in many ways, including their participation in the sport of volleyball. The year 1973, especially, was pivotal for women's volleyball. It was the inaugural year for both the women's World Cup and the Junior World Championships. The 26,000 spectators who came to watch the Women's World Championship in Brazil set a new record for attendance at a women's event.

Women's professional beach volleyball began to take off in the 1980s. In 1986, the Women's Professional Volleyball Association (WPVA) was created. And in 1987, the first Women's Professional Volleyball event was held. Finally, in 1999, beach volleyball was added to the Olympics.

The future of women's volleyball is bright. The year 1999 also saw the formation of the United States Professional Volleyball League, a professional league for women players. The intention of the league is to make women's volleyball as popular a spectator event as the Women's National Basketball Association (WNBA) has made women's basketball.

The Basic Rules

Initially, volleyball consisted of nine innings and any number of players could play. The object was to serve and return the ball over the net, keeping it traveling from team to team without hitting the floor. If a team failed to return a serve, the serving team would score a point.

The rules have been refined over the years. Today, teams are made up of either two people—in beach volleyball—or six people—in indoor volleyball. The object of the game is to keep the ball from touching the ground or floor on your side of the court and then send it back to your opponent's side. Strategically, you want to send the ball over the net in such a way that it is difficult for your opponent to return it. If they miss, can't return it, or send it out of bounds, your

Beach vs. Indoor Volleyball

	Beach	**Indoor**
Court Size	26'6" x 59'	26'6" x 59'
Number of hits	Three hits to return the ball and no player can hit the ball twice in a row	Three hits to return the ball and no player can hit the ball twice in a row
Court	Outdoors, on sand at least 40 centimeters deep	Indoor, hardwood floor
Number of players on each team	2	6

team will get a point or the serve (depending on how the game is being scored, which we will discuss shortly). Spiking the ball is the most recognizable way to accomplish this goal.

Each team can touch the ball only three times when it is on the team's side of the court (this includes blocking contact), and no player can touch the ball twice in a row unless she is blocking the ball at the net. (Blocking is singled out as an exception in the rules because it is not a manner of hitting the ball, like passing or spiking.)

Strategies

There are three basic strategies for indoor volleyball play: the 4-2, the 6-2, and the 5-1.

The 4-2 is the most common set-up; a team with four hitters and two setters. The setters play opposite each other, meaning that if one setter is in the middle of the front row, the other is in the middle of the back row. In this configuration, one setter will always be in the front row to set for two hitters. The setter in the back row plays as a passer.

The 6-2 means that there are six hitters and two setters, but this does not mean that there are eight players on the court. It means that the two setters act as hitters as well. This is a little more complicated. After the ball is served, the setter in the back row moves to the front and the other setter remains in front, too, but moves to the right side of a hitter.

How Volleyball Has Changed

	Then	Now
Court Size	25' x 50' (into two 25' x 25' sides)	26'6" x 59' (FIVB, USAV, CBVA, WPVA)
Net Height	6'6"	Girls 10 years old and under: 6'6" Girls 10 to 12 years old: 7' Women: 7'4 1/8" (WPVA, FIVB, USAV, CBVA)
Ball	Not less than 25" in circumference and no more than 27", weighing between 9 and 12 oz.	About 26" in circumference and weighing between 9 and 10 oz.

Volleyball players want to send the ball over the net so that it is difficult for opponents to return it.

This means that there are four people in the front row and only two in the back. The goal of this set-up is to have most hitters and blockers in the front row. It is very important that every player knows where she is supposed to be; otherwise, the court will not be sufficiently covered.

The 5-1 is the most complicated strategy. It consists of five hitters and only one setter. The setter in this case does not do double duty as a hitter as well. In this strategy the setter must be fast, precise, and in very good shape. An advantage to this strategy is that the players get to know the setter's style; however, it can also leave the front row with only two hitters instead of three (like in the 6-2).

Scoring

The most common way for games to be scored is called sideout scoring. In sideout scoring, only the team that is serving the ball can score a point. The nonserving team simply wins back the serve—and thus has the chance to score—if the serving team fails to return the ball in bounds. A team wins when it scores fifteen points with at least a two-point advantage. For example, a team can win if the score is 15–13, but not if the score is 15–14. In the event of a 16–16 tie, the team that scores the seventeenth point wins the game. The team that wins three games first, wins a match.

There is another type of scoring called rally-point scoring. In rally-point scoring, the team that wins the rally (the back and forth of the ball) wins a point, regardless of whether that team served or not. And when the team wins the point, it also gains possession of the serve (if it did not already have it).

If both teams have won an equal number of games, rally-point scoring is used for the deciding game in a match in which sideout scoring had been used for all previous games. This type of scoring was also recently (in 1999) adopted by USA Volleyball, the national governing body for the sport of volleyball in the United States. Rally-point scoring can also be used for an entire match, in which case the team that scores twenty-five, with a two-point minimum advantage, wins each nondeciding game. In the event of a deciding game, the victor is the team that scores fifteen points with a two-point minimum advantage. With a rally-point scoring system, there is no scoring cap—meaning that the game continues for as long as is needed so that there is more than a one-point difference in the score.

Positions

While some volleyball team members may be excellent setters, spikers, or servers, every member of the team plays all the different areas of the court. Each time a team wins the serve, the players rotate one space clockwise, thus changing each player's position. While players physically rotate positions on the floor, each skill position (the setter, hitter, or blocker) has certain strengths that the coach knows he or she can rely on.

Often, taller girls on the team are setters, blockers, and spikers. This is because they don't have to jump as high to reach the top of the net. Shorter girls also can play these positions if they have explosive jumping power. Jump training is something that can help you become an effective blocker.

Being agile and stable are two characteristics of good hitters. It doesn't matter if you are short or tall, as long as you can sense where the ball is directed and make sure you can get under it to pass it to your setter. As we'll discuss later, there are many ways for you to work on your coordination and agility.

A good volleyball player is able to sense where the ball is headed, and can get under it in order to pass it to her setter.

Athlete Profile: Flo Hyman

Flo (Flora) Hyman (1954–1986) was one of the most influential volleyball players in the history of the game. A 6'5" three-time All American, she is widely considered to be the best volleyball player of all time. Known not only for her excellent spiking and defensive skills, but also for her personality and charm, she was the first American woman to be voted to the All-World Cup volleyball team. An all-around player, she led the U.S. Women's Olympic team to a silver medal in the 1984 Olympics.

After the Olympics, she went to Japan to play professional volleyball there. During a match in 1986, she collapsed and died. She was thirty-one. Her death was a result of Marfan's syndrome, a genetic heart disorder that predominantly affects tall and thin individuals.

She was inducted into the Volleyball Hall of Fame in 1988. Her dedication to female athletes in all sports is honored with the Flo Hyman Memorial Award, which is given annually by the Women's Sports Foundation to athletes who have captured her "dignity, spirit, and commitment to excellence."

Equipment and Cost

It doesn't have to cost a lot to play volleyball. All you need is a pair of volleyball shoes and a volleyball. Regulation size and weight volleyballs come in both leather and vinyl. Volleyballs start at around $30 for synthetic leather or vinyl and $40 for real leather. When getting shoes, you need a combination of cushioning, stability, and lateral, or side-to-side, support. Shoes come in high, medium, and low top. Many major athletic footwear makers make specific volleyball shoes, and prices start at around $50.

How to Get into the Game

There are usually many opportunities to get involved in volleyball through your school. Volleyball is often offered in gym class, where the basic positions and rules are explained and practiced. Many schools also have their own teams that play other schools for standings in an organized, official league. Schools might also have club teams, which are more informally organized and often do not require try-outs. Playing on these more casual teams gives you a great opportunity to learn the game and get experience so you will have the skills needed to make your school team.

If your school doesn't offer volleyball, you might try the local YWCA or community center. You can contact the U.S. Youth Volleyball League to learn where the teams are in your area. The regional office of USA Volleyball also has a list of club teams.

2 Training

Volleyball requires specific skills combined with athleticism. Every player on the team should be able to execute all of these skills since they may, at some time, play every position. It is the years of practice and experience that develop the difference in performance. All movement and action should start from the ready position—feet apart, knees bent, eyes forward, ready to move in any direction.

Serving

Serving is the action that gets the ball going. It is a common way to score points because many times a serve can be so powerful it can't be returned by the opponent. When you score a point like this, it's called an "ace."

The overhand serve is the one most often seen in the Olympics and professional sports. Standing at the end line, toss the ball two to three feet above your head and slightly in front of you. Make sure you don't touch the end line before making contact with the ball; otherwise, you will lose the serve. Take a step forward while shifting your weight from your right to left foot, if you are right-handed. Arch your back and bend your right arm to bring it up from behind your head. Hit the ball with your hand and make sure your arm follows through.

The first way to work on your serve is to practice the form as outlined above. Once you get the hang of it, try choosing a target and directing your serve toward it. For a greater challenge, put a time limit on yourself—see how many good serves you can do in a minute.

Defense: Hitting the Ball

When receiving a serve, you'll need to know how to pass or "bump" the ball. When bumping, you want to place the ball high enough for a teammate to set it so that the third hitter can spike it. In making a good pass you can set up a play that might win you a point or the serve.

When you pass, the ball hits the widest part of your forearm, right between the wrist and elbow. Don't swing your arms at the ball. Instead, move your arms by shrugging your shoulders in the direction you want the ball to go.

You can hold your hands in three different ways. You can cup them together and cross your thumbs in the center. You can make a fist with your writing hand and put your other hand over it, making sure that both thumbs are touching and side by side. Or, you can lay one hand into the palm of the other and cross your thumbs. Your thumbs are important because if they are in the right position, your arms are in the right position.

A simple drill for working on your bump is to bump the ball repeatedly off your own arms. You can also get a couple of teammates together to play "keep it up," passing the ball from player to player without letting it drop or having to set it, which leads us to our next type of pass, setting.

Setting is an overhand pass. You should start in the ready position facing where you want the ball to go. With your hands above your head and your fingers spread, make a triangle with them by having your thumbs and index fingers touch. You don't want your hands too far above your head, just slightly above and in front of your face. Make sure that you get underneath the ball and that your elbows and knees are bent. When the ball touches your fingers, extend your arms and legs to move the ball.

Make sure that both hands touch the ball at the same time; otherwise, the referee might count it as a double or a mis-handle. A double could result in your team losing possession of the ball if you have the serve or in your opponents being awarded a point if they have the serve. Also, don't let the ball touch the palm of your hand—otherwise, you will be called for "pushing," which is a way of controlling the ball unfairly.

You can practice the skill of setting by doing a variation of the "keep it up" drill. Try lying on your back with your arms extended upward and your elbows facing outward. Set the ball upwards and see how long you can do it. You can do this standing as well.

Spiking

One of the more difficult, but useful skills to acquire is hitting, more commonly known as spiking. Spiking is a quick offensive movement. Done properly, it is a difficult or impossible hit to return. A setter will position the ball so that you, the spiker, can take a couple of steps forward and then jump up with both feet. As you jump, you should swing both arms forward. Pull your hitting arm back with the elbow and hand around shoulder height. Your hand should be open, not in a fist. As you swing your

To set the ball, stand at the end line and toss the ball a bit above your head and in front of you. Step forward and hit the ball with your hand. Don't forget to then follow through with your arm.

Spiking is a quick offensive movement that is hard for the opponent to return.

hand and arm over your head, the heel of your hand will make contact first, followed by your palm, and then fingers (which snap through the ball). Your contact point should be just in front of your hitting shoulder and as high as possible.

Spiking is best practiced by having a partner repeatedly set the ball for you. It can also be done as a group drill with one person setting and the rest coming up, one after another, to spike.

One of the best ways to stop a spike is by blocking. To be a good blocker, a good sense of timing and strong jumping legs are essential. To develop your blocking skills, make sure that you keep your eye on the spiker. You'll have to watch her eyes, shoulders, and hands to figure out when and where she's going to spike. You don't want to jump too soon and miss your opportunity. Stand close to the net, but not so close that you touch it. When you sense she's about to spike, jump straight up from both feet with your arms extended upwards. If your timing is right, the ball will bounce straight back into your opponent's court. If you're not quite that successful, you'll slow the ball down enough so that one of your teammates can get to it.

A sense of timing is developed through practice, but you can always work on your jumping. If you have a net you can use, practice approaching it with a couple of steps and then jumping as though you were going to block the ball. Another drill is to jump upward as if to block, shooting your arms upward, and repeating as many times in a row as possible. As soon as you touch the ground, jump up again. With each jump, you should be reaching above the volleyball net. Once you can no longer reach that high, stop.

Conditioning

Along with practicing specific skills, you need to work on your general conditioning or fitness, which will enhance your ability to perform. Without strong legs, how will you jump high? Without strong arms, how will you hit the ball powerfully? And without endurance, how will you play strong for the entire game? An average game can last anywhere from sixty to ninety minutes, and while the players aren't in constant motion, they do need to be ready to perform well throughout that entire time. They need to have cardiovascular, local muscle, and strength endurance. Developing overall endurance, both muscular and cardiovascular, is an important step in training for volleyball.

Cardiovascular endurance means that your heart can deliver blood to your muscles and that your muscles can use it efficiently and quickly. Any activity that keeps your heart rate up for at least twenty minutes at a time, like running or rollerblading, is a good way to develop that kind of endurance. Working on your cardiovascular conditioning three times a week is a good formula for increased endurance.

Developing muscle endurance increases your muscles' ability to perform an action continuously over an extended period of time, and allows you to give your all, over and over. Volleyball requires not only sustained effort, like that required for moving around on the court, but also short bursts of action, like jumping to block or spike the ball. Cycling, swimming, or running will help your muscles develop sustained endurance, while practicing your jumping will help enable your muscles to perform quick actions repeatedly.

It's not all about endurance, though. You also need strength, flexibility, and coordination (which includes balance and agility, the ability to move quickly and gracefully).

An overall strength-training program, which includes working your arms, legs, and upper body, can help you in many ways. To develop a good weight-lifting program, consult with your coach or a trainer at your gym.

Flexibility allows your body to perform a wide range of movement and helps you stay injury free. People who can bend at the waist and touch their hands to the floor have a nice degree of flexibility. Incorporating a stretching regimen

Volleyball players often participate in other activities, such as cycling, swimming, or running, to keep themselves in top physical condition.

or yoga into your training will help increase your range of motion. Also, flexibility can help improve your coordination.

Coordination is very important, particularly in volleyball. Often, you will have to sprint to get to the ball while preparing to return it and, hopefully, seeing a good place to direct it. That's a lot of different things going on at the same time. Coordination makes it possible for you to do all those things. Agility is the ability to change your direction of movement quickly, like sprinting to the ball and then back to position to be ready again. Balance allows you to stay on your feet.

Stretching

Stretching is a critical part of any conditioning regimen. Stretching primes your muscles for the workout ahead, which helps prevent injuries that stem from putting too much stress on unprepared or already tight or fatigued muscles.

Proper stretching begins after you have warmed your muscles up and raised your heart rate. You can run for a few minutes, do some jumping jacks, or jump rope to get the blood flowing.

The following are just a few exercises you can do to stretch your muscles and get ready to play. Hold the stretches consistently for about thirty seconds. Don't bounce. Repeat each of them at least twice on each side.

Calf Muscles

Find a wall, a tree, or some other sturdy structure. Stand about two feet away from it. Step back about a foot with your right foot. Bend your left knee and lean forward, pushing slightly on the wall in front of you. Your right leg should be straight and you should feel a stretch in the right calf. If you need to, you can move you left foot forward a bit to get more of a stretch. Hold this for thirty seconds and then switch feet.

Hamstrings

Sit on the floor with your right leg extended and your left leg bent under you, with your foot touching your buttocks. Slowly begin to slide your hands down the straight leg. You should start to feel a

Stretching your muscles prepares them for workouts and helps prevent injuries that may happen if you stress tight and tired muscles.

Stretching your hamstrings, as pictured here, helps prepare your legs for running and jumping.

stretch in the back of that leg. Hold this position for thirty seconds. Don't round your lower back; try to keep it fairly straight, bending at the waist. Return to a sitting position when done. Switch sides and repeat.

Quadriceps

Stand with your hips facing forward, bend your right knee back, and grab your right ankle with your right hand. Keep your hips facing forward and your right knee pointing at the floor. You should feel a mild stretch along the front of your right leg. Hold this for thirty seconds and then switch legs.

Shoulders

Since your shoulders will see a lot of action in a volleyball game, it is not a bad idea to do both of the stretches outlined here before you begin practicing. You should feel this first stretch in your shoulder. Rotate your shoulders forward (like shrugging) ten times and then backward ten times.

This second stretch is great for your triceps. Raise your right arm, bend it at the elbow so that your right hand is behind your head and your right elbow is pointing toward the sky. Take your left hand and gently pull your right elbow further behind your head, toward the left. Let your right hand slide down your back. Keep your shoulders down and relaxed. When you begin to feel the stretch in your muscle, hold for thirty seconds. Switch arms.

Training and conditioning shouldn't stop when the volleyball season ends. Find another sport to play in the off-season, or continue with your basic conditioning plan. It's a great way to stay fit, and gives you a good start for the next volleyball season.

Injuries

Although volleyball is not a dangerous activity, it can lead to injuries. Injuries suffered by volleyball players usually occur in the ankles, knees, shoulders, or lower back.

Ankle and knee injuries often occur when two or three players make contact or collide. This generally happens near or underneath the net. As players scramble to take or resume positions, paths sometimes cross and bodies fall. You can also pull or tear muscles and ligaments while diving for the ball.

As far as your choice of shoes, there is no clear-cut case for the low, mid, or high top when it comes to prevention. Some players will wear some kind of ankle support. Almost 85 percent of all sprains result from falling on the outside of the foot, causing the sole to turn inwards.

There are three degrees of sprains. The first involves the stretching of ligaments. These are usually mild and you'll

experience some pain, point tenderness, swelling, and limited disability. The second degree is more serious, as it involves the tearing of the ligaments. You will feel more pain and be limited in your movement. You won't be unable to put any weight on the ankle. The third degree, and most serious, is when the ligaments are ruptured. Severe pain, joint

Falling on your knees to get a ball can cause strains, so some players wear kneepads or braces to avoid knee injuries.

instability, and disability are just some of the signs. A doctor should attend to second and third degree sprains.

Any ankle sprain will bruise and swell within twenty-four hours. Re-member "RICE"—Rest, Ice, Compression, and Elevation—and you'll aid your own recovery. Be sure to ice any ankle sprain regularly in twenty-minute increments during the first forty-eight to seventy-two hours. How long you must rest depends upon the severity of the sprain. If you feel minor discomfort and can walk on it after twenty-four hours, you might be able to practice your setting or passing, but don't go too fast or you'll likely increase the damage. Unfortunately, once you hurt your ankle it's often susceptible to more injuries. To keep your ankle from reinjury, you might consider an ankle brace to add stability.

The other major joint injury occurs in the knees. Knee injuries come not only from contact with other players, but from the repeated running, jumping, and turning that players do during a game. Falling on your knees to get a ball can also cause a strain. Knees are very complicated joints, and any injury or pain in them should be treated seriously. Some players will wear kneepads or braces to help avoid knee injuries.

Your shoulders will see a lot of action in a volleyball game. Good conditioning, strength training, and stretching can help prevent injuries in the shoulder area. However, even then, not everyone can avoid getting hurt. Some of the symptoms of a shoulder injury are a numbing pain throughout the arm, unusual sounds (like cracking or popping) when you rotate your shoulder, pain when doing something simple like throwing a ball, and an inability to raise your arm above ninety degrees.

Doctors can treat shoulder injuries in a number of ways, depending upon the severity. One thing is certain, though, shoulder injuries require a lot of rest—anywhere from eight to ten weeks or more. You might also get a rehabilitation program set up for you by a physical therapist. This can help you gradually regain full use and movement in your shoulder.

Lower back injuries stem from the repeated stress placed on that area (the lumbar spine) by spiking and serving. This area bears the weight of your body as you move, and the arching and the twisting of the back can result in injury. Lower back injuries may manifest as spasms, pinched nerves, or herniated discs. If you experience back pain and it doesn't go away within a day or so, see your doctor.

You can see that injuries can be serious if not treated carefully. It doesn't make you a tougher athlete if you suffer silently through pain, all the while making your injury worse. Many female athletes feel like they have to prove that they are tough. In reality, it takes a smart and tough woman to listen to her body and do what's right for it.

If you do experience injury, it can be a time to appreciate volleyball from the sidelines. You can watch how your team performs, support them, and think about how your contribution can improve. Also, use this time to explore other parts of your life so that you are refreshed and hungry to play when you are healed.

Injuries are not the only event that can sideline you; overtraining is another aspect of sport that can keep you out of the game. It is not uncommon for enthusiasm and the desire to improve to lead to too much training. That is why part of being a good athlete is being able to listen to your body and know when it needs rest and attention.

Overtraining

Training is important, but it is possible to train too much, or overtrain. There is a limit to your body's ability to adapt to and endure training, especially when you increase the intensity. Your body needs rest and time to recover after hard workouts. Muscles need to rebuild and flush out toxins.

Overtraining can occur when your level of intensity is too high, too early in your training. It can happen when you don't give yourself enough time to rest, or when you train without considering other stresses in your life. Maybe your workouts aren't getting more difficult, but you have a big term paper due in a week. All stresses in your life affect your body and your training. When you overload your body with stress, you are prone to overtraining. And overtraining can be as detrimental to your performance and progress as injuries.

If you overtrain, you'll feel tired, you won't be able to play as well as you did before, and you will feel as though there is nothing more you can do. The harder you train, the slower you seem to get. The only way to recuperate is by resting. You don't have to be totally inactive, but you should try something different and less stressful on your body, like leisurely swimming or taking long walks.

The Mental Game

Just as your body needs conditioning to perform well, so does your mind. For years, professional athletes have used visualization and goal setting as tools to help them perform better. If you're physically prepared but your head is not in the game, you will not perform your best.

To be part of a successful team, athletes and their coaches need to work together, both during games and in practice.

First of all, it is important to have a good attitude. Approach volleyball with a desire to learn and improve. It's tough not to compare yourself to others, but you should concentrate on just doing the best that you can do. When you give your all, you should be happy with yourself, even if your team didn't win the game or someone else played better.

If you're having difficulty with a particular move or skill, it often helps to think about it, to visualize it. Imagine yourself executing a great overhand serve. One of the benefits of visualization is that you can slow down, repeat, or even stop the action in your head. This allows you to see how you stand, the position of the ball in the air, how you make contact, and the final follow-through. By visualizing it, you can learn it mentally and then put it into practice physically.

Setting goals is also a great mental exercise. By setting goals you can help yourself stay motivated. Goal setting also helps by focusing your attention and relieving stress.

You can set goals for yourself as well as for your team. Maybe you want to perfect your overhand serve, and you want to help the team communicate better. These are two very realistic goals. You can work on your serve through practice and visualization, and you can foster communication on your team by communicating yourself.

Make sure that your goals are realistic. If you have long-term goals like being on the starting line-up, make sure you have some intermediate ones as well that will both help you reach your long-term goal and give you a sense of satisfaction and accomplishment along the way. Maybe what you need to be on the starting line-up is that overhand serve.

Finally, set goals for yourself in the other areas of your life. This helps establish a balance. Setting goals for school or other activities helps keep things in perspective.

Achieving balance isn't always easy, particularly when you're excited about something new, such as volleyball. But balance allows you to focus on other things that are important in your life—like friends, school, family, and other hobbies, such as reading or music. It's great to give your new interest your all, but the other areas of your life shouldn't have to suffer. Spending time away from volleyball is also important because it gives you both a physical and a mental break. A break can take the shape of a holiday or playing a different sport in the off-season. When you take a break and then return to play, you're refreshed. If you don't do other things too, volleyball can become mundane and even feel like a chore.

Nutrition

How many times have you heard that your body is like a machine and needs fuel? Well, it's true, and the right kind of fuel can help your body perform better and longer. A cola and a doughnut might help you make it through the morning, but once the initial sugar-and-caffeine rush wears off, you will be groggy and tired again.

Nutritionists don't all agree on the best diet. Some favor a diet high in carbohydrates, such as pasta, grains, and bread. Others prefer a diet high in protein from foods such as fish, meat, legumes (beans), and nuts. As a growing woman and athlete, it's best to make sure you get a good balance of both of these, plus fruits, vegetables, and dairy products. Women need lots of calcium to help build bone mass, especially because many women suffer from osteoporosis, a loss of bone density which causes bones to become brittle and break easily—and it's not something that just happens to "old ladies." Whether you get your calcium from a glass of milk, some yogurt, or calcium supplements, it's important to get

As a woman and an athlete, you should eat a healthy diet of fruits, vegetables, grains, proteins, and dairy products.

enough (1,200-1,500 milligrams per day for adolescents and young adults from eleven to twenty-four years of age).

Following a balanced diet will ensure that you get all the nutrients your body needs. Neglect an area like vegetables and you'll miss out on a great source of vitamins and minerals. Protein, which can be found in soy products and meat, will help build and repair tissue, as well as provide vitamins and minerals. And grains are an excellent source of fiber and carbohydrates for energy.

Unfortunately, it's common for women athletes to become obsessed with their weight and body size. In a sport like volleyball, girls often feel self-conscious because of the fairly revealing uniforms. This can result in what is known as the female athlete triad—eating disorders, low bone density, and missed periods. These three things can develop when you try to control your eating in such a way that you don't get enough nutrients. Being healthy and strong is one of the most important things for an athlete. Poor eating habits or eating disorders destroy both.

It's also important to drink lots of water. Your body is made up of more water than anything else and you need to keep it that way. Dehydration can be a very serious problem for athletes. Water keeps you going and keeps your system functioning smoothly. And athletes need to drink even more water because of how much they lose by sweating.

3 Competition

The purpose of practice and conditioning is to be ready to play your best on game day. Competition is a very healthy aspect of sports, as long as you learn to take it in stride and keep it in perspective. We all want to win, and that desire is often what motivates us to work our hardest. But sometimes, even when you work hard and play well, you don't win.

Keeping competition in perspective means realizing that the outcome of the game is not entirely under your control. Because of this, it is important to focus on the process of competing rather than just on the outcome. Focus on what you and the team did well, and praise others and yourself for a job well done. Also, be aware of where you or the team did not do well, and focus on improving those weaknesses when you are at practice.

In volleyball, you usually face competition once a week at a scheduled match, or during a weekend tournament where you play a number of games in a series of elimination rounds. Before a game, you need to do just a little extra preparation. Make sure that you're well rested the day before. Don't have a long conditioning session or increase your weights right before a game. Your muscles will be too busy recuperating to give their all. You can still do an easy workout. Your coach will probably arrange to have your workouts follow this plan, but you also must know what works best for you. You need to pay attention to your own body and know how to best prepare yourself to perform your best on game day.

Mentally, you will also need to relax. Focus on your own performance within the team. Don't stress yourself out by worrying about what you can't do or how you might mess up. Instead, think about doing everything to the best of your ability. Remember how you've set the ball for your teammates or how well you served in other matches.

Team Play

Keep in mind that you are part of a team. If a team works as a unit, it can go much farther and be much more successful than any individual alone. Liz Masakayan, professional women's beach volleyball player, sums it up when she says, "A volleyball team is a lot like a marriage: It requires trust, responsibility, and problem solving. It's an intense bond you

Competition is a natural part of sports, but it's good to maintain a healthy attitude toward winning and losing.

have with your teammates: You work, travel, and room together, and as in any relationship, there are problems that need to be solved."

To work as a team, players need to be able to communicate and trust each other. When a serve comes to your side, a player should call for it and others should be confident in her ability and not second-guess her. If the setter is in position, she should communicate to her teammates so that they'll pass to her. Communicate not just to direct and claim, but also to encourage each other.

Good Sportswomanship

It's easy to get caught up in the spirit of the moment and become so focused on winning that you forget about being a good sport. You may want to hate your opponents and say some nasty things to them, but they're out there just like you, and they, too, are doing their best. Good sportswomanship means focusing on doing your best, enjoying the game, and enjoying the competition. Calling a girl on the other team an "ugly cheater" does nothing to enhance your own performance. It brings you down, as well. Instead, let their tough play inspire you to play better.

Good sportswomanship doesn't always prevail, and trouble can brew between opposing teams. The best thing to do is just walk away. You might be angry at a loss or you might be celebrating loudly over a win, but saying something rude or

Players on a team should be able to communicate and trust one another. A team that works together can be successful and have fun.

gloating to an opposing player doesn't help make the loss easier or the victory sweeter.

Team Relations

You may not always get along with all of your teammates. Nobody says you have to be best friends, but you should try to respect each other. At the very least, it's important to keep the lines of communication open. You might need your coach to help if there are two of you who won't talk to each other. It's normal for there to be disagreements or disappointments, but they shouldn't hang over you too long. Letting them stew affects the entire team. You could end up dreading practice or games. Conflict is natural—deal with it.

You might also experience conflict with your coach. Think about what the basis of your conflict is—do you think he or she is pushing you too hard? Does he or she say things about your performance that make you mad? Do the two of you disagree about strategy? You don't have to think that your coach is the greatest, but you should respect him or her. A coach's job is to bring out the best in each player and to bring all of the players in the team together. Sometimes harsh words are spoken, but the intention usually isn't to hurt. If you feel like comments are inappropriate or wrong, talk to your coach. Maybe he or she does not realize that his or her comments were hurtful. Conflict is almost always best dealt with by communicating. By confronting the situation, you may be able to come to a peaceable understanding.

Competition is a great part of team sports, especially when everyone is working together and keeping their focus on playing the game. Every team has its share of wins and losses, but every athlete is a winner when she plays to the best of her abilities.

4 Opportunities for Volleyball Players

Over the past few years, women's professional sports have grown and are beginning to be appreciated for the spectator draw that they are. We now see WNBA games televised, and more and more opportunities are available for female athletes. Many girls today don't have to see their athletic careers end after college or the Olympics. Volleyball is no exception. There are professional, national, and international leagues for both beach and indoor volleyball. The United States Professional Volleyball League was formed in 1999 as a professional league for women volleyball players. Currently, it is in the planning stages for an inaugural season scheduled for January 2002. The league plans to have six to ten teams with a season that lasts from January through May. With ambitious expansion plans, the league hopes to have thirty-two teams by 2015.

Beach volleyball players also have professional opportunities available to them. Women's professional beach volleyball is organized in the United States by Beach Volleyball America (BVA), and internationally by the Federation Internationale de Volleyball (FIVB). Both host and arrange tournaments and competitive events for women beach volleyball players.

You don't have to choose between sports and academics, either. The passage of Title IX ensured greater scholarship opportunities for women athletes all over the country. There are over 950 colleges and universities that have National Collegiate Athletic Association (NCAA) teams, and almost 300 of those are Division I teams. A 1999 report by the NCAA noted that in 1997–1998, athletic scholarships for women had increased over 140 percent since the 1991–1992 school year. Today, women receive more scholarship money than men in many Division I sports, including volleyball. Scholarships are offered at schools across the country, from Ivy League colleges to state universities.

You don't have to be a professional player to continue playing as an adult. There are plenty of recreational leagues for adults, and some of the resources in this book will help you find teams. Recreational leagues do not lack for competition or commitment to the sport, so you don't have to worry about losing your edge. A love of the game developed now can last well into your adult life.

Volleyball can help you develop your body, your understanding of teamwork, and your sense of competition and achievement. Keeping strong and healthy in both your mind and body is something that will benefit you throughout your life, and volleyball can help you accomplish these things. You don't have to wait for another gym class to try volleyball again, you can go out and make your own opportunity. You might get hooked.

1895 — Volleyball is invented in Holyoke, Massachusetts. By the 1990s, volleyball is the second-largest participation sport in the United States, with more than 42 million participants. There are indoor and outdoor competitions for boys and girls, men and women, and co-ed teams.

Early 1920s — Origin of beach volleyball in Santa Monica, California.

1965 — The California Beach Volleyball Association is founded.

1964 — Volleyball is added to the Olympic Games.

1970 — The United States' Mary Jo Peppler is voted the outstanding volleyball player in the world at the International Games in Bulgaria.

1975 — Olympian and U.S. national team member Debbie Green becomes volleyball's youngest All-American at sixteen years of age.

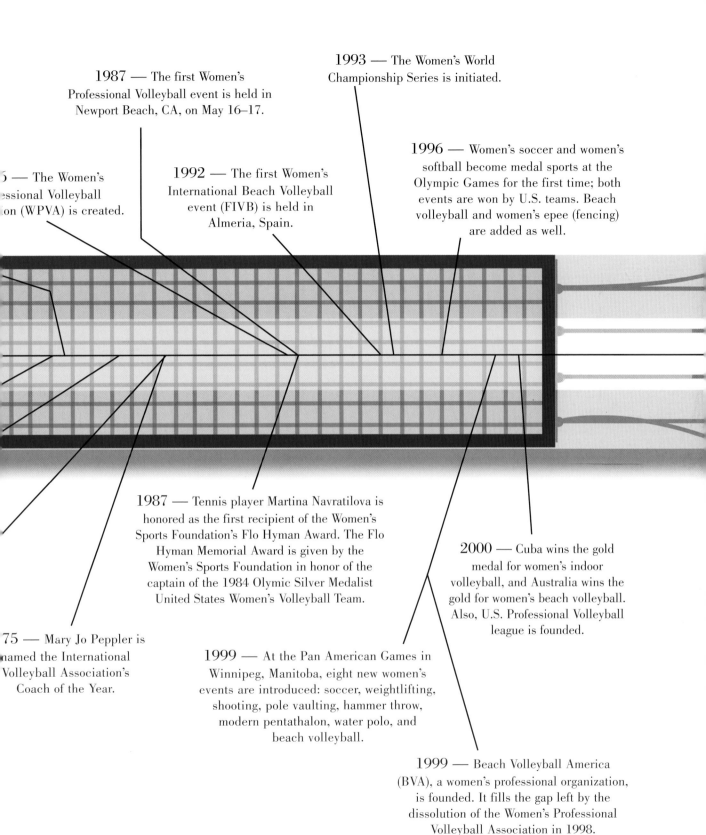

1987 — The first Women's Professional Volleyball event is held in Newport Beach, CA, on May 16–17.

1993 — The Women's World Championship Series is initiated.

1996 — Women's soccer and women's softball become medal sports at the Olympic Games for the first time; both events are won by U.S. teams. Beach volleyball and women's epee (fencing) are added as well.

5 — The Women's essional Volleyball on (WPVA) is created.

1992 — The first Women's International Beach Volleyball event (FIVB) is held in Almeria, Spain.

1987 — Tennis player Martina Navratilova is honored as the first recipient of the Women's Sports Foundation's Flo Hyman Award. The Flo Hyman Memorial Award is given by the Women's Sports Foundation in honor of the captain of the 1984 Olymic Silver Medalist United States Women's Volleyball Team.

2000 — Cuba wins the gold medal for women's indoor volleyball, and Australia wins the gold for women's beach volleyball. Also, U.S. Professional Volleyball league is founded.

75 — Mary Jo Peppler is named the International Volleyball Association's Coach of the Year.

1999 — At the Pan American Games in Winnipeg, Manitoba, eight new women's events are introduced: soccer, weightlifting, shooting, pole vaulting, hammer throw, modern pentathalon, water polo, and beach volleyball.

1999 — Beach Volleyball America (BVA), a women's professional organization, is founded. It fills the gap left by the dissolution of the Women's Professional Volleyball Association in 1998.

Glossary

cardiovascular Relating to the heart and blood vessels.

compression Squeezing or pressing together.

conditioning Getting physically ready.

defense Plan or action to keep the other team from scoring.

endurance Withstanding long periods of stress.

gender Classification of sex (male or female).

lateral Pertaining to side or side-to-side movement.

ligaments The tissue that joins bones or cartilage, or supports organs and muscles.

meditation The act of reflecting or contemplating.

motivation Incentive or psychological push.

muscles Tissues that cause body movement.

nutrients Substances found in foods that nourish the body.

offensive The means used in an attempt to score.

ratio The relationship in quantity or size of two things.

recuperate To restore health and strength.

rehabilitation To restore regular activity after an injury.

scholarships Financial aid given to students.

stability Resistance to sudden change or action.

strategy Planning; a plan of action.

visualization Forming a mental picture or image.

For More Information

Association of Volleyball Professionals (AVP)
330 Washington Boulevard, Suite 600
Marina Del Rey, CA 90292
(310) 577-0775
Web site: http://www.avptour.com

California Beach Volleyball Association (CBVA)
2646 Palma Drive, Suite 325
Ventura, CA 93003
(800) 350-CBVA (2282)
(805) 642-CBVA (2282)
 Web site: http://www.eteamz.com/cbva

United States Youth Volleyball League
12501 South Isis Avenue
Hawthorne, CA 90250
(310) 643-8398

(888) 988-7985
Web site: http://www.volleyball.org/usyvl

USA Volleyball
715 South Circle Drive
Colorado Springs, CO 80910
(719) 228-6800
(888) 786-5539
Web site: http://www.usavolleyball.org

Volleyball World Wide
P.O. Box 1872
Cupertino, CA 95015-1872
(408) 358-8622
E-mail: volleyballorg@hotmail.com
Web site: http://www.volleyball.org

Women's Sports Foundation
Eisenhower Park
East Meadow, NY 11554
(516) 542-4700
(800) 227-3988
Web site: http://www.WomensSportsFoundation.org

In Canada

True North Volleyball Magazine
47 Harmony Hill Crescent
Richmond Hill, ON L4C 8Z4
(905) 508-8134
Web site: http://www.tnvmag.com

Volleyball Canada
5510 Canotek Road, Suite 202
Gloucester, ON K1J 9J5
(613) 748-5681
Web site: http://www.volleyball.ca

Web Sites

Federation of International Volleyball (FIVB)
http://www.fivb.org

Volleyball Magazine On-line
http://www.volleyballmag.com

Volleyball Stuff
http://www.volleyballstuff.com

Women's Professional Volleyball Association (WPVA)
http://www.volleyball.org/wpva/

For Further Reading

Andes, Karen. *A Woman's Book of Strength*. New York: Berkley Publishing Group, 1995.

Bertucci, Bob, and James Peterson. *Volleyball Drill Book: Game Action Drills*. Indianapolis, IN: Masters Press, 1992.

Bertucci, Bob, and James Peterson. *Volleyball Drill Book: Individual Skills*. Indianapolis, IN: Masters Press, 1992.

Crisfield, Deborah W. *Winning Volleyball for Girls*. New York: Facts on File, 1995.

Gozansky, Sue. *Championship Volleyball Techniques and Drills*. West Nyack, NY: Parker Publishing Co., 1983.

Jensen, Julie. *Beginning Volleyball.* Minneapolis, MN:
Lerner Publications, 1995.

Jensen, Julie. *Fundamental Volleyball.* Minneapolis, MN:
Lerner Publications, 1995.

Kiraly, Karch, and Byron Shewman. *Beach Volleyball.*
Champaign, IL: Human Kinetics, 1999.

Lucas, Jeff. *Pass, Set, Crush: Volleyball Illustrated,* 3rd ed.
Wenatchee, WA: Euclid Northwest Publications, 1993.

Pearl, Bill, and Gary T. Moran. *Getting Stronger: Weight
Training for Men and Women,* rev. ed. Bolinas, CA: Shelter
Publications, 2001.

Reece, Gabrielle, and Karen Karbo. *Big Girl in the Middle.*
New York: Crown Publishers, 1997.

Selinger, Arie, and Joan Ackerman-Blount. *Arie Selinger's
Power Volleyball.* New York: St. Martin's Press, 1987.

Shewman, Byron. *Volleyball Centennial: The First 100 Years.*
Indianapolis, IN: Masters Press, 1995.

Thigpen, Janet. *Power Volleyball for Girls and Women*, 2d ed. Dubuque, IA: W. C. Brown Co., 1974.

Viera, Barbara L., and Bonnie Jill Ferguson. *Volleyball: Steps to Success*, 2d ed. Champaign, IL: Human Kinetics, 1996.

Wise, Mary, ed. *Volleyball Drills for Champions*. Champaign, IL: Human Kinetics, 1999.

Index

W

women professional athletes/sports, 6, 10, 18, 20–21, 35, 42, 47–49

Women's National Basketball Association (WNBA), 10, 47

Women's Professional Volleyball Association (WPVA), 10

Women's Sports Foundation, 18

Women's World Championship, 9

women's World Cup, 9, 18

Y

YWCA, 19

About the Author

Claudia B. Manley is a writer who lives in Brooklyn, New York, with her son, partner, and cat.

Photo Credits

Series Design and Layout

Danielle Goldblatt